Defining
MOMENTS
OVERCOMING CHALLENGES

Bethany
HAMILTON

Follow Your Dreams!

by Michael Sandler

CONSULTANT
Sunshine Makarow
Publisher, Surf Life for Women Magazine

BEARPORT
PUBLISHING

Credits
Cover and title page, © AP Photo/Ronen Zilberman; 4, © AP Photo/The Garden Island, Dennis Fujimoto; 5, © Michael Patrick O'Neill /Photo Researchers; 6R, © Giulio Marcocchi /NewsCom; 6L, © Sportschrome/NewsCom; 7, © Tony Arruza/Corbis; 8, © Jim Russi Photography; 10, © Jeannie Chesser; 11, © Gallery 808; 12, © Dan Jenkins Jr.; 13, © Awe F'Shore Photography; 14, © Terry Lilley; 15, © Michael Latronic; 16, © Jeff Rotman/Photo Researchers; 17, © AP Photo/The Garden Island, Dennis Fujimoto; 18, © Raymond Gehman/Corbis; 19, © Courtesy of Wilcox Hospital; 20, © AP Photo/Dennis Fujimoto; 21, © Sportschrome/NewsCom; 22, © Robert Hogan; 23, © AP Photo/Steamboat, Larry Pierce; 24, © Gallery 808; 25, © AP Photo/West Hawaii Today, Michael Darden; 26, © Joob/phuketboardriders/Saltwater Dreaming; 27, © AP; Photo/Lucy Pemoni.

Publisher: Kenn Goin
Project Editor: Adam Siegel
Creative Director: Spencer Brinker
Photo Researcher: Marty Levick
Original Design: Fabia Wargin

Library of Congress Cataloging-in-Publication Data
Sandler, Michael.
  Bethany Hamilton : follow your dreams! / by Michael Sandler.
    p. cm. — (Defining moments. Overcoming challenges)
  Includes bibliographical references and index.
  ISBN-13: 978-1-59716-270-8 (library binding)
  ISBN-10: 1-59716-270-1 (library binding)
  ISBN-13: 978-1-59716-298-2 (pbk.)
  ISBN-10: 1-59716-298-1 (pbk.)
  1. Hamilton, Bethany. 2. Women surfers—Hawaii—Kauai—Biography—Juvenile literature. 3. Amputees Hawaii—Kauai—Biography—Juvenile literature. 4. Shark attacks—Hawaii—Kauai—Biography—Juvenile literature. I. Title. II. Series.

  GV838.H36S26 2007
  797.3'2092—dc22

                                    2006006941

For more information, write to Bearport Publishing Company, Inc., 101 Fifth Avenue, Suite 6R, New York, New York 10003. Printed in the United States of America.

10 9 8 7 6 5 4 3 2 1

Table of Contents

Halloween

For most children, Halloween is the time to go trick-or-treating. For Bethany Hamilton, it was a chance to catch the perfect wave.

Surfing was Bethany's **passion**. The 13-year-old girl had plenty of talent. Each night she dreamed of becoming a **pro** surfer.

Bethany Hamilton

So at sunrise on October 31, 2003, Bethany was already at the beach. She pushed her board into the surf. Floating in the crystal-clear Hawaiian water, she let her left arm dangle below the surface. Bethany was waiting for the next wave.

Instead, out of nowhere, came a giant gray blur. Bethany felt a tug. The water turned red with blood.

Bethany was attacked by a tiger shark that was about 14 feet (4 m) long. Tiger sharks are the most dangerous sharks in Hawaiian waters.

A tiger shark

A Family of Surfers

If anyone was born to surf, it was Bethany Hamilton. She jokes that she was born with salt water in her **veins**. In fact, Bethany grew up in a family of surfers. Her parents loved the sport so much that they moved to Hawaii and never left. The waves for surfing there were just too good.

Bethany's parents

Cheri Hamilton

Tom Hamilton

6

A surfer riding a huge wave in Hawaii

Surfers need waves to **propel** them across the water. Around the islands of Hawaii there are plenty of waves. They are often very big, too. So Hawaii is the place to be for surfers. People have been surfing in the area for more than 1,000 years.

Bethany was born in Hawaii. She was just five years old when she first started surfing.

Keeping Up

Bethany was the youngest of the family's three kids, and she was the only girl. Her brothers, Timmy and Noah, loved sports. They played fast and tough. To keep up, Bethany learned to be tough as well.

Like Bethany, Noah is a surfer. Timmy, however, prefers bodyboarding. This sport is similar to surfing except that bodyboarders usually lie down on their boards rather than stand on them.

Bodyboarder in Hawaii

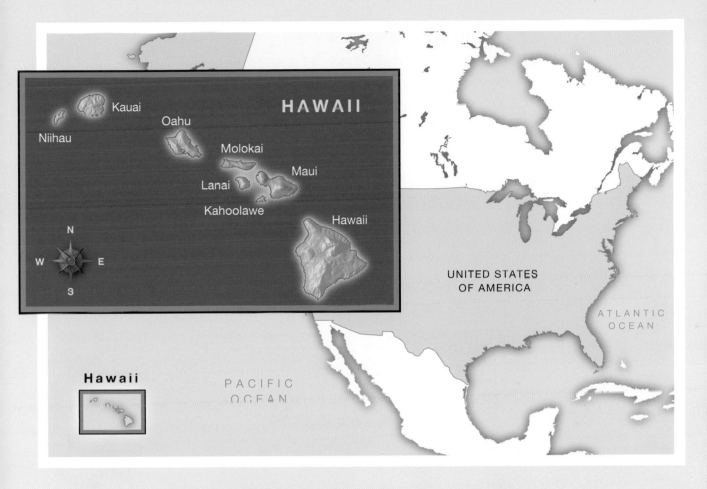

Hawaii is made up of islands in the Pacific Ocean. They are about 2,500 miles (4,023 km) from the U.S. mainland. Bethany grew up on the Hawaiian island of Kauai (kuh-WYE-ee).

Bethany often got knocked down in soccer, and tackled in football. Yet it didn't bother her. She loved sports and she loved **competing**. Most of all, she loved to surf.

By the age of seven, Bethany was entering surfing contests. Unlike other young surfers, she didn't need a parent's help to get her board out into the water. Bethany could catch her own waves!

Winning

When Bethany was eight years old, she scored her first big win. It was at the Rell Sunn Menehune (MEH-nay-hoo-nay) Surf Contest, a competition for kids under 13 years old.

Bethany was nervous. Many great surfers had entered. The waves were huge. One girl wiped out and ended up with a deep cut across her throat.

The Rell Sunn surfing competition began in the 1970s. These children were some of the first surfers to compete in it.

Makaha (MAH-kah-hah) Beach, site of the Roll Sunn contest, is famous for its 15-to-30-foot (4-to-9-m) fierce waves. In fact, "Makaha" is the Hawaiian word for "fierce."

Surfer at Makaha Beach

Bethany knew she wouldn't have an easy ride. Yet she put aside her fears. The young surfer hit the waves and won one **heat** after another. Bethany took first place in two categories. She was proud of her trophies. Best of all, though, she had won two new surfboards!

Dancing in the Waves

As Bethany grew older, more wins followed. By the time she entered her teens, she was one of the country's top **amateur** surfers. Her family came to every contest, giving her tips and cheering her on. They supported her whether she won or lost.

Surfers at the 2002 National Championships in San Clemente, California

In summer 2003, Bethany took second place at a national championship contest in San Clemente, California. To do so, she beat many surfers twice her age!

Bethany riding a wave

Winning wasn't everything, though. Bethany just loved surfing. She loved the feel of dancing in the waves. To Bethany, surfing was the "force that moves you body and soul."

On days when she couldn't surf, Bethany barely felt alive. That's why on Halloween morning she was so **anxious** to head for the beach.

Clear Skies

Bethany hadn't surfed in days. The weather had been awful—rain and more rain. On Halloween morning, Bethany woke up and listened for the sound of raindrops. She didn't hear any rain. She jumped up and grabbed her bathing suit.

Tunnels Beach on the North Shore of Kauai is considered one of the best surfing spots in Hawaii.

Bethany and her friends were known as the Dawn Squad because they liked to surf early, just when the sun was coming up.

It was still dark when Bethany and her mom reached the beach. Sadly, the water was calm. There were no waves. They decided to look for another spot. At Tunnels Beach, they found more calm water. The pair decided to head home.

Just then, however, a pickup truck pulled up. Out came Bethany's best friend, Alana, and her family. Bethany decided to stick around.

Bethany's best friend, Alana Blanchard

Shark Attack

Soon the surfers were floating in the sea, waiting for a wave. None of them saw the shark coming. When it struck, Bethany felt no pain, just a **massive** tug. She turned, staring at the jaws of the beast.

The attack lasted a few seconds. Bethany didn't scream. She was dazed, but she knew right away she was in trouble.

A tiger shark's saw-edged teeth make the animal deadly.

Bethany looked at her left arm. It was gone!

"Get to the beach," she told herself. In seconds, Alana's father, Holt, was by her side.

He tried to stop the bleeding by making a **tourniquet** from his shirt. Then he pulled Bethany toward the shore.

The shark attack occurred nearly a quarter of a mile (.4 km) offshore. Paddling back took almost 15 minutes.

Bethany's surfboard after the attack

Life or Death

On shore, a crowd gathered around Bethany. Now she finally felt the pain. She passed in and out of **consciousness**. She felt so cold! People wrapped her in towels.

Soon an ambulance arrived. The **paramedics** thought that she might die. She'd lost so much blood and it was nearly an hour's drive to the hospital.

The island's twisting roads slowed down Bethany's rush to the hospital.

Kauai's Wilcox Memorial Hospital, where Bethany was taken after the attack

The ambulance driver pressed down on the gas pedal. How much time did Bethany have?

At the hospital, **surgeons** cleared out the operating room so Bethany could be rushed in. They gave her blood. They cleaned her terrible **wound**. Bethany was going to survive!

Still the Same?

Bethany stayed in the hospital for one week. She needed time to heal and regain her strength.

Her family was with her constantly. Other visitors came to see her, too. They looked at her bandages. Bethany saw many of their faces fill with **pity**.

Don't feel sorry for me, she wanted to say. I'm still the same.

One of the first things Bethany asked while recovering in the hospital was, "When can I go surfing again?"

Bethany being interviewed about two weeks after the attack

Bethany and her parents

Yet at times during the weeks after the accident, even Bethany had her doubts. She was shocked the first time she saw her naked arm. It was a stump covered in stitches. "I look like Frankenstein's monster," she thought to herself.

A New Life

While Bethany felt the same inside, she was discovering that her life had changed. Everyday tasks suddenly became very difficult. How could she get dressed with one arm? How could she button her shirt or tie her shoes? To peel an orange she would have to hold it between her feet.

This statue was made in honor of Bethany's refusal to give up her dream of surfing.

Bethany knew she needed to forget about ever surfing again. It was completely out of the question—except that Bethany couldn't forget.

The attack hadn't **diminished** her love for the sport. She wasn't ready to give up her dreams. Less than a month after the injury, Bethany was back up on her surfboard.

Bethany returned to surfing on the day before Thanksgiving in 2003.

Bethany snowboarded in Colorado less than four months after the shark attack.

Riding the Waves Again

Getting out into the waves wasn't easy for Bethany anymore. Paddling with just one arm was difficult. Standing up on the board was equally tough. Still, catching that first wave after the accident made everything worthwhile. Bethany remembered, "I rode it all the way to the beach, and after that, I just had . . . tears of happiness."

Learning to paddle with only one arm was not easy.

Today, Bethany is competing once again. She had five top-three finishes by November 2005. Other surfers can't believe the way she's bounced back.

"It's amazing to me," says Keala Kennelly, one of the world's top pros. "I really don't think I could do it."

On January 10, 2004, Bethany surfed in her first competition since losing her arm. Only ten weeks had passed since the shark attack.

As Long As I Can

Can something good come out of something terrible? Bethany thinks so. She still dreams of surfing victories, but now she's got other dreams, too.

Bethany wants to make a difference in people's lives. She wants to help others learn to deal with pain and loss. Most important, Bethany wants to encourage people to follow their dreams, no matter how hard it seems.

In 2005, Bethany went to Thailand. She met with children who lost their parents in the **tsunami**. Later that year, she helped raise funds for victims of Hurricane Katrina.

Bethany in Thailand

What does the future hold for Bethany? Only one thing is certain: her life will include plenty of surfing. "I've been surfing since I was five," she said, "and I'll be surfing until however long I can."

Just the Facts

■ In the 2005 National Scholastic Surfing Association (NSSA) National Championships, Bethany won first place in the Explorer Women's division.

■ Shark attacks can be deadly, but luckily they are not very common. Americans are 30 times more likely to be killed by a lightning bolt than a shark and about 15,000 times more likely to die in a car accident.

Timeline

Here are some important events in Bethany Hamilton's life.

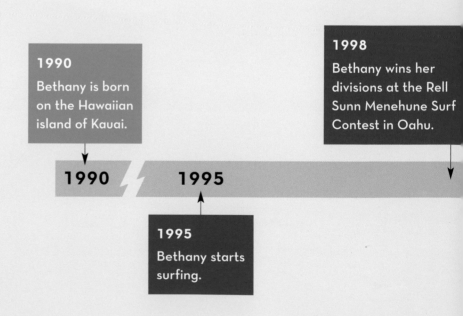

1990
Bethany is born on the Hawaiian island of Kauai.

1998
Bethany wins her divisions at the Rell Sunn Menehune Surf Contest in Oahu.

1990 **1995**

1995
Bethany starts surfing.

■ Who was in the operating room when Bethany arrived at the hospital? By coincidence, it was Bethany's dad. He was waiting to undergo knee surgery. They rushed him out to make way for his daughter.

■ In ancient Hawaii, surfing was known as "the sport of kings." The best surfboards and surfing spots were reserved for Hawaiian royalty.

■ Bethany is a hero to many people. Who is her hero? It's not a surfer. It's Father Damien. His full name is Joseph Damien de Veuster. From 1873 to 1889, he helped people in Hawaii who were suffering from **leprosy**.

2005
June: Bethany wins her division at the NSSA National Championships.
August: Bethany travels to Thailand to help children who suffered in the tsunami that hit South Asia on December 26, 2004.

2003
October: Bethany loses her arm in a shark attack.
November: Bethany surfs again.

2000

2005

2004
January: Bethany resumes competitive surfing.
August: Bethany takes first place at a National Scholastic Surfing Association contest in Hawaii.

Glossary

amateur (AM-uh-chur) an athlete who does not receive money for competing; an athlete who is not a professional

anxious (ANGK-shuhss) eager

competing (kuhm-PEET-ing) playing or performing against others in order to win

consciousness (KON-shuhss-ness) the state of being awake, alert, and able to think

diminished (duh-MIN-isht) lessened, made smaller

heat (HEET) a single round of a contest

leprosy (LEP-ruh-see) a disease that attacks a person's skin, muscles, and nerves; it can cause loss of feeling and movement of body parts

massive (MASS-iv) large

paramedics (pa-ruh-MED-iks) people who are medically trained to respond to emergencies and take care of people until they arrive at a hospital

passion (PASH-uhn) something a person likes more than anything else

pity (PIT-ee) the feeling of sorrow for another person

pro (PROH) short for "professional"; an athlete who gets paid to play sports

propel (pruh-PEL) move or push forward

surgeons (SUR-juhnz) doctors who perform operations

tourniquet (TUR-nuh-ket) a tight bandage wrapped around a limb to lessen the bleeding from a wound

tsunami (tsoo-NAH-mee) a huge wave or group of waves caused by an underwater earthquake or volcano

veins (VAYNZ) vessels inside a person's body through which blood is carried back to the heart

wound (WOOND) an injury in which a person's skin is cut

Bibliography

Hamilton, Bethany, with Sheryl Berk and Rick Bundschuh. *Soul Surfer: A True Story of Faith, Family, and Fighting to Get Back on the Board.* New York: Pocket Books (2004).

Honolulu Star-Bulletin

www.bethanyhamilton.com

www.cnn.com

Read More

Berger, Melvin, and Gilda Berger. *What Do Sharks Eat for Dinner?: Questions and Answers About Sharks.* New York: Scholastic (2000).

Green, Naima. *Surfing: Rules, Tips, Strategy, and Safety.* New York: Rosen Publishing Group (2004).

Kampion, Drew. *Waves: From Surfing to Tsunami.* Layton, UT: Gibbs Smith (2005).

Peterson, Christine. *Extreme Surfing.* Mankato, MN: Capstone Press (2005).

Learn More Online

Visit these Web sites to learn more about Bethany Hamilton and surfing:

www.bethanyhamilton.com
www.cybersydney.com.au/kids/sar/surf.html
www.timeforkids.com/TFK/news/story/0,6260,583739,00.html

Index

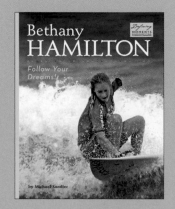

About the Author

MICHAEL SANDLER lives and writes in Brooklyn, New York. He has written numerous books on sports for children and young adults.